ANCIENT CIVILIZATIONS

Greece

By Christy Steele

STECK-VAUGHN
ELEMENTARY · SECONDARY · ADULT · LIBRARY

A Harcourt Company

www.steck-vaughn.com

Copyright © 2001, Steck-Vaughn Company

ISBN 0-7398-4147-5

Library of Congress Cataloging-in-Publication Data is available upon request.

Printed and bound in the United States of America

10 9 8 7 6 5 4 3 2 1 W 04 03 02 01

Photo Acknowledgments
Archive Photos, 28
Corbis/David Lees, 9; Archivo Iconografico, 10, 13, 33; Peter Harholdt, 14;
    Gianni Dagli Orti, 16; Bettmann, 34, 37
Photo Network, title page; Phyllis Picardi, 24; Bill Bachmann, 40, 43
Root Resources/Paul Hodge, 30, 38
Unicorn Stock Photos/Jean Higgins, cover
Visuals Unlimited/Jeff Greenberg, 19, 47; Barry Slaver, 23; Irwin "Bud"
    Nielsen, 26

Contents

LEGEND

⬤ Ancient and
    Modern Greece

⬤ Cities

▢ Water

▲ Mountain

▲ Mount Olympus

Troy

Aegean Sea

*Ionian
Sea*

Delphi

Athens

Corinth

Sparta

RHODE

*Mediterranean
Sea*

CRETE

Knossos

Ancient Greece was at its peak from about 776 to 31 B.C. During this time, people from many Greek cities formed a great **civilization**. A civilization is an advanced society. Life could be different in each Greek city. But all Greek people shared a common language. They created new ideas in building, writing, medicine, and government. Some Greek ideas still affect our world today.

Greek civilization began on mainland Greece and western Turkey. Greek people needed more land to grow enough crops to feed everyone. So, they started new cities in Italy, Sicily, and small islands in the Aegean and Mediterranean Seas.

GREEK TIMELINE

3000 B.C.-1100 B.C. Bronze Age	c. 1500-1120	•Mycenaean Civilization
1100 B.C.-776 B.C. Dark Ages	c. 1100	•Doric Invasion of Greece
	c. 1050-950	•Greek colonization of Asia Minor (western coast of Turkey)
	c. 900	•Beginning of the rise of the city-sta
776 B.C.-479 B.C. Archaic Age	776	•Olympic Games established
	c. 750	•Greek colonization of Southern Ital and Sicily begins
	c. 650	•Greek colonization around the Black Sea begins
	336-323	•Alexander the Great rules; unites city-states into one country and takes over many new lands
	323	•Alexander the Great dies
479 B.C.-323 B.C. Classical Age	490-479	•Persian War
	431-404	•Peloponnesian War (Athens and allies vs. Sparta and allies)
	404	•Athens loses Peloponnesian War to Sparta
323 B.C. - 31 B.C. Hellenistic Age	323-280	•Alexander the Great's generals fight for power
	280-160	•Spread of Greek ideas to lands Alexander conquered

c. = circa (about)

City-States

The land of Greece shaped Greek civilization. Mountains or the sea separated settlements. Each settlement grew into its own **city-state**. A city-state is a tiny nation built around a central town. There were hundreds of city-states in Greece. Each city-state ruled itself. For much of Greek history, city-states never joined into one country. In fact, the city-states were almost always fighting wars with each other.

Early Greek History

During the Bronze Age, Mycenaean people lived in Greece. They created an **alphabet** and a writing system. Historians are not sure what happened to the Mycenaeans. Historians are people who study history. Some historians think that the Dorian people from northern Greece fought them and won.

The Dark Ages was the second period of Greek history. It lasted from about 1100 to 776 B.C. The reason it is called the Dark Ages is because the people forgot the writing system and other ideas of the Mycenaeans. Around 776 B.C., small villages formed into city-states.

Periods of Greek History

The Archaic Age lasted from 776 to 479 B.C. During this time, the Greeks created an alphabet and writing system. Greek authors wrote long poems called **epics**. They made coins to use as money. Greek settlers started new cities in Ionia. The Persians tried to take over Greece around 480 B.C. But many of the city-states worked together to fight the Persians. The Greeks won the war.

The Classical Age lasted from about 479 to 323 B.C. Greek people created many new works of art and literature. The city-state Athens started a new kind of government called **democracy**. In a democracy, people shaped government by voting on new rules. At the end of this time, Alexander the Great of Macedonia fought and took over Greece. He made the city-states join into one country. Greece was the most powerful at this time.

This is a statue of Alexander the Great when he was a young man.

The Hellenistic Age lasted from about 323 to 31 B.C. During this time, Greek ideas spread throughout lands Alexander had taken over. When Alexander died, his generals fought for control of Greece. As a result, the places Alexander took over broke into three kingdoms. A different king ruled each kingdom.

This pottery shows a man driving a vehicle called a chariot. In early Greece, kings supplied their city-states with horses and chariots.

Government

The kinds of government in Greece changed throughout the centuries. In early Greece, kings ruled each city-state. They came into power because they had a great deal of goods and property. They gave good gifts to their people and other leaders.

During the Classical Age, Athens became the first democracy. Democracy means rule by the people. Citizens of Athens could vote on how to run their city-state. A citizen was a free male from Athens who was over 18 years old. Women, **slaves**, and people from other countries were not citizens. They could not vote or own property. A slave is a person owned by another person.

The citizens gathered together in a meeting called the Assembly to make decisions. There, they voted on how to run the country.

A council of 500 people headed the Assembly. They were picked from among the 10 **tribes** of Athens. A tribe is a large group of families. Each tribe picked 50 people to be on the council. The council helped decide what the Assembly would vote on.

Under democracy, Athens became one of the most powerful city-states. Athens forced most of the other city-states to copy its way of ruling. They became democracies, too.

Athens and Sparta

Athens and Sparta were the two most powerful city-states during the Classical Age. Athens was a democracy. But Sparta was an **oligarchy**. In an oligarchy, only a few people rule. A small number of wealthy, powerful male citizens ruled Sparta.

In Athens and other city-states, men learned to become soldiers from age 18 to 20. They were asked to fight only if Athens went to war. Athens had a strong navy with many ships. Athens made **allies** with other city-states. Allies have special agreements to help each other.

Spartan society was based on war. In Sparta, males learned to become soldiers starting at age seven. Early in its history, Spartans took over Messenia. They made the people of Messenia slaves. These slaves were called **helots**. Spartans formed a powerful army to control the helots and fight other city-states. Like Athens, Sparta also made allies with other Greek city-states.

This pottery shows Spartan men fighting soldiers from other city-states. Spartan men served in the army from age 20 to 60.

Around 430 B.C., some Spartans felt Athens was growing too powerful. Sparta and Athens and their allies went to war. The war was called the Peloponnesian War. It lasted for about 27 years. Sparta won the war.

This picture shows some different shapes of Greek pottery.

Greece and the World

Greek people traded with many different peoples around the world. Except for Sparta, the most powerful city-states were built near the sea. These city-states had good **harbors**.

A harbor is a place with deep water where people can anchor ships. Ships from other countries stopped in Greek harbors to trade goods.

Greek ships also left Greece to trade. Greek people needed to buy grain. Farmers could not grow enough grain to feed all the Greek people. Greek ships sailed as far away as Egypt. They traded olive oil and **pottery** for grain, perfume, and costly silk cloth.

Sometimes Greek city-states fought with other people over land. If the city-state won, they made some of the other people slaves. They brought the slaves back to their city-state to work.

Through trading and wars, the Greek people learned much about other people of the time. Ideas from other countries sometimes affected Greece. For example, Greek traders brought back artwork from Egypt. Some artists used ideas from Egyptian art to make their own Greek art.

This pottery shows what Greek shepherds looked like. Shepherds care for animals.

Daily Life in Greece

Greek people had different roles. The most powerful people in Greek city-states were male citizens. They were in charge of money, made laws, and went to war.

Women in Greece lived most of their lives inside their houses. They left the house to get drinking water. Young girls learned skills, such as cooking and making cloth.

Many Greek slaves worked inside people's houses. They served food and cleaned. Others farmed or worked in mines.

Metics were people from foreign places who lived in Greece. Many metics were artists or scientists. Metics could not own property or vote. But they did have to pay taxes.

Greek Dress

Men and women wore a straight **chiton**. A chiton was a long, rectangular piece of cloth that was cut in two. It was held together at the shoulders by pins. Some chitons had pins that ran all the way down the arms. A cord or string around the waist served as a belt.

The chiton could be different lengths. Women wore long, ankle-length chitons. Men, children, and slaves often wore knee-length chitons. Chitons were sometimes bright colors, such as red or purple.

Greeks sometimes wore himations over their chitons. A himation was a long piece of cloth draped across the shoulders and arms.

Single women wore their hair long with headbands, barrettes, or combs in their hair. Married women used nets, ribbons, and combs to pile their long hair on their heads. Slave women had short hair.

Rich people often wore jewelry. Men wore gold or silver rings. Women wore necklaces, bracelets, and large, dangling earrings.

This statue shows how single Greek women styled their hair.

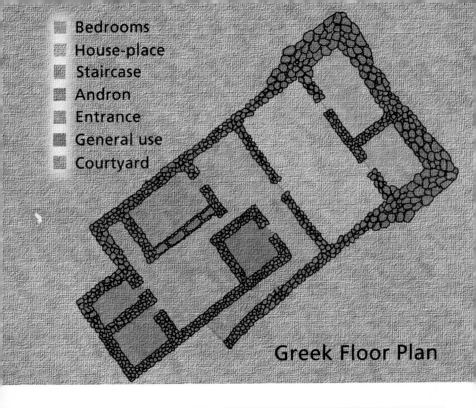

- Bedrooms
- House-place
- Staircase
- Andron
- Entrance
- General use
- Courtyard

Greek Floor Plan

> This illustration shows the common placement of rooms in a Greek house.

Greek Homes

Greek homes were simple, small buildings. The number of floors and rooms a house had depended on the owner's wealth.

Many Greeks built their homes on a layer of stones. They used mud bricks to form the walls. They cut small window openings near the tops of the walls. People closed the windows with wood shutters. Sometimes they coated the inside and outside of the walls with plaster. They put colorful hangings on the walls. Clay tiles covered the roofs.

Greeks built their houses around an open courtyard. Rich homes had a fountain or well for drinking water in the courtyard. Poor homes often did not have wells.

The lower level had an andron, or dining room, close to the front door. Men had drinking parties in the andron. There were often rooms for cooking and for women to work. The upper level had bedrooms.

Greek people did not have much furniture because wood was very costly. There were usually couches in the andron. A Greek couch was a lot like a bed. It was low and flat. One side was raised slightly. Greeks had low tables. They pushed the tables under the couches when they were done using them. Greeks also sat on low, three-legged stools.

Greek Food

Most Greeks were farmers. They were able to grow some grain, such as wheat and barley. Greeks used the grain to make bread and soup.

Since the ground was dry, there were only a small number of plants for animals to eat. They did not raise many animals for food. Most Greek households raised one or more goats. They milked the goats. They drank some of the milk and made the rest into cheese. Some people also raised chickens and ate the eggs. Seafood was common because many Greek city-states were near the sea. Fishers caught many kinds of fish.

Olives were another common food. Olive trees grew well in the dry, rocky soil of Greece. Greeks ground olives into olive oil and used the oil to cook with and clean themselves. They also traded olive oil with other peoples around the world.

The Greeks also grew grapes. They mixed the juice from the grapes with water. The

The Greeks used oil from olives to fuel their lamps. The lamps burned oil.

mixture was left in bowls until it turned to wine. Wine was the most important drink.

Greek people used honey to sweeten their food. They raised bees to get honey. The Greeks ate sweet fruit, such as figs or pomegranates, for dessert.

Temples were one kind of public building that the Greeks built.

Greek Culture

A people's **culture** is their way of life. A culture includes ideas, customs, and traditions. These things were slightly different throughout Greece. But all Greek people expressed themselves through the things they did and the things they made.

Greeks expressed pride in their own city-states by building large public buildings and holding sporting events. In sporting events, athletes from different city-states competed against each other. One famous sporting event was the Olympic Games. It was first held in 776 B.C. In today's Olympic Games, most of the sports and the way they are played are very different.

> The Parthenon in Athens took 15 years to build.

Religion

Religion was an important part of Greek culture. Greek people believed that gods and goddesses ruled the world. Gods or goddesses are powerful beings with special powers. They believed that the gods lived on top of a tall mountain called Mount Olympus. Each god or goddess was in charge of a different thing. For example, Aphrodite was the goddess of love. Ares was the god of war.

People told stories of the gods and goddesses to explain the world around them. These stories are now called myths.

Greek people created statues of their gods and goddesses to honor them. They built **temples**. A temple is a building used for worshiping gods. At certain times of the year, they held huge celebrations to honor the gods and goddesses. The Greeks gave offerings of money, food, and animals to their gods and goddesses.

Each city-state had a special god or goddess to protect it. The city-state built temples for their god or goddess. Athena was the goddess of wisdom and war. She was the goddess of Athens. The people of Athens named their city-state after her. They built a huge marble temple called the Parthenon for her. They made a large gold and ivory statue of Athena and put it inside the Parthenon.

Greek artists often carved pictures like this
on the walls of public buildings.

Greek Art

Each city-state had craftspeople. These
people made many things, including shoes,
pottery, and sculptures. They also painted
and carved stone and wood. They sold their
goods in a marketplace called the agora. The

28

agora was set up in a large, cleared place inside the town. Craftspeople set up booths. They took down the booths when the city-state needed the space to hold large meetings.

Athens and Corinth were most famous for their pottery. They shaped clay into pots, bowls, cups, jugs, plates, and vases. Then they painted the pottery with pictures of everyday life or stories about the gods and goddesses. The pottery was then placed into hot ovens and baked until it was hard.

Greek artists also created sculptures. Some of the sculptures were made of stone, and others were made of bronze. The male figure was a popular subject. Artists tried to make their sculptures look as real as they could. Many of the bronze statues do not exist today. In later times, people melted the statues and used the bronze to make other things.

Greek metal workers formed pictures in metal. They made fancy coins and jewelry, such as rings and earrings.

> Corinthian columns are supporting the frame of this ancient Greek building.

Greek Architecture

Although individual Greek homes were small, people built huge temples and public buildings. Architecture is a style and way of building. Greek architecture used columns.

There were several kinds of Greek columns. Doric columns were thick. They had simple

30

tops. Ionic columns were thinner than Doric columns and had scrolls at the top. Less often, Greeks used Corinthian columns. These columns had fancy tops carved with leaves.

Greek temples and public buildings were built of stone. They had statues on the inside and outside. Stone carvings of gods and goddesses decorated the walls and ceilings. Greek temples also had outdoor altars. An altar is a place where people put offerings.

Greek Theater

Theater was an important part of Greek life. Wealthy city-states built huge theaters on hillsides. Stone seats lined the hill. At the bottom of the hill was a stage.

Plays were either very funny or very sad. They were often about heroes, average men, or the gods and goddesses. Some plays made fun of important people.

Male actors performed all the parts in the plays. It was against the law for women to act. Actors wore masks to show their moods and whether the character was male or female.

Greek Schools

Learning was important to the ancient Greeks. The sons of rich citizens had teachers when they were seven years old. But poor children could not afford teachers. Their parents taught them what they could at home. Most girls did not attend school. Their mothers taught them to make cloth and cook at home.

Students learned how to read and write the Greek alphabet. They wrote on small wood pieces that were covered with wax. They wrote with a tool called a **stylus**. They used the pointed end of the stylus to write letters or numbers in the wax. They used the flat end of the stylus to rub out mistakes.

Students also learned math. They used an **abacus** to count. An abacus has a square frame with wires that run from one side to the other. Round beads for counting are on the wires. The students moved the beads to do math problems.

This pottery shows a Greek student receiving a dancing lesson.

Students also learned how to play musical instruments. They played flute-like pipes or the lyre. The lyre was like a small harp. It had seven strings attached to a turtle shell.

Physical fitness was important to Greeks. In the afternoons, students went to special places called gymnasiums to exercise.

The famous Greek doctor Hippocrates wrote guidelines for surgery.

What Did the Greeks Do?

Greek people did many important things. They came up with new ideas that helped shape later civilizations.

Greeks made discoveries in medicine. The city of Epidaurus had a famous temple built to honor the god of medicine, Asclepius. People from around the world went to the Epidaurus temple or places like it for treatment. Priests who served Asclepius treated sick people with different diets, baths, and exercise.

One famous Greek doctor was Hippocrates. Today, Hippocrates is often called the father of modern medicine. He learned that the parts of a person's body work together. He wrote more than 50 books about medicine.

Science and Writing

Greek scientists figured out some main rules of math. Pythagoras studied the triangle. He found the formula that helped people figure out the length of the sides of a right-angled triangle.

Greek scientists also came up with new ideas. The great thinker Aristotle is given credit for creating the scientific method. A method is a way of doing something. Using this method, scientists gather facts about something. They use the facts to make an educated guess about why or how something happens. Then, they test their guess to see if it is true.

Other Greek scientists studied the stars and planets. Most scientists of the time believed that Earth did not move and that the Sun circled Earth. But an astronomer named Aristarchus suggested that Earth moved around the Sun. Another astronomer named Anaxagoras thought that the Moon only reflects light from the Sun.

▲ Aristotle started many schools and even
taught Alexander the Great.

There were many famous Greek writers.
Herodotus is called the father of modern
history. He wrote books about Greek history
and the Persian Wars. The writer Thucydides
wrote the history of the Peloponnesian War.
Aristophanes, Euripides, and Sophocles wrote
plays for Greek theater. Homer was a poet.

This Greek statue is made of bronze.
Romans also made many statues
of bronze.

How We Know about Greece

The ancient Greeks were taken over by Rome about 300 years after Alexander the Great died. By then, Greece had been divided into smaller pieces ruled by different kings. Roman armies took over the Greek kingdoms one by one. Greece became a part of Rome.

Today, we know much about Greek culture because Romans copied the culture instead of destroying it. Roman people used Greek ideas to build their own civilization. Roman buildings and sculptures were a lot like Greek buildings and sculptures. Romans even built temples and worshiped gods and goddesses like the Greeks.

Archaeologists can learn about Greek theater by studying theater ruins.

Greek Sites and Artifacts

Archaeology shows us much about the Greeks. Archaeology is the study of ancient remains. Archaeologists study objects made by ancient Greeks. The objects show what life was like during that time.

People have found many Greek **artifacts**. An artifact is an object that was used by humans in the past. Some of the most valuable artifacts are Greek pottery. Archaeologists study the drawings on the pottery. The drawings show what daily life was like. For example, one vase shows a picture of two workers picking olives. One man is in the tree shaking the branches with sticks to make the olives fall. This pottery showed archaeologists how the Greeks gathered olives.

Archaeologists today also learn about Greek life by studying the remains of Greek buildings. Small buildings, such as everyday houses, no longer stand. Mud brick does not last long. But many parts of the stone buildings still stand. Archaeologists study the remains to learn about Greek building methods. Some archaeologists are trying to reconstruct the buildings to make them look as they did in ancient Greece.

Greece in the Modern World

Greek ideas still shape the world today. Many buildings are built with columns like ancient Greek buildings.

People use Greek discoveries. Scientists use the scientific method to study the world around them. Students learn the Pythagorean Theorem in math classes today. Doctors still learn the Hippocratic Oath in medical school.

People read and study Greek stories. Books by Herodotus teach about Greek history. Students study Greek myths and plays. Actors sometimes perform Greek plays.

Modern artists are often inspired by Greek art. They draw or paint pictures of life in ancient Greece. They may draw pictures of scenes from myths. They copy Greek pottery.

One of the most important ideas from ancient Greece was democracy. Many countries have based their governments on the principle that everyone should be a part of government. The United States' government was based on this idea.

Today, visitors to Greece often visit the remains of ancient temples.

Glossary

abacus (AB-uh-kuhss)—a frame with sliding beads on wires that is used for counting

ally (AL-eye)—a person or country that has a special agreement to support another

alphabet (AL-fuh-bet)—all the letters of a language arranged in order

archaeology (ar-kee-OL-uh-jee)—the study of ancient remains

artifact (ART-uh-fakt)—an object that was used by humans in the past

chiton (SHEYE-tuhn)—a piece of clothing made of a long, rectangular piece of cloth that was cut in two and held together at the shoulders by pins

city-state (SIT-ee-STATE)—a tiny nation built around a central town

civilization (siv-i-luh-ZAY-shuhn)—a highly developed and organized society

culture (KUHL-chur)—the way of life, ideas, customs, and traditions of a group of people

democracy (di-MOK-ruh-see)—a way of ruling a country where people vote on how to run their country

epic (EP-ik)—a long story, poem, or movie about heroic adventures and battles

harbor (HAR-bur)—a place where ships anchor or unload their goods

helot (HEE-laht)—a slave owned by a Spartan

oligarchy (ohl-i-GAHR-kee)—a way of ruling where a small group of people have control

pottery (POT-ur-ee)—objects made of baked clay

slave (SLAYV)—a person owned by another person and thought of as property

stylus (STEYE-luhs)—a tool with a pointed end and a flat end that is used for writing

temple (TEM-puhl)—a special building used for worshiping gods

tribe (TREYEB)—a large group of families

Internet Sites

Ancient Greece
http://home.freeuk.net/elloughton13/greece.
htm

Electronic Passport to Ancient Greece
http://www.mrdowling.com/701greece.html

The Greeks
http://www.pbs.org/empires/thegreeks/

**Voyage Back in Time: Ancient Greece
and Rome**
http://www.richmond.edu/~ed344/webunits/
greecerome/

Useful Addresses

American Classical League
Miami University
Oxford, OH 45056-1694

**Classical Association of the Middle West
and South**
Department of Classics
Randolph-Macon College
Ashland, VA 23005

> ▼ Today, this carving from the Parthenon is
> in a museum.

Index